UNINTERRUPTED WORSHIP

DORRETTE AYENSU

Copyright © 2025 by Dorrette Ayensu

All rights reserved under United States of America Copyright Law. None of the contents and/or cover may be replicated or transmitted in any form including electronic, photocopy, and recording or any other, entirely or in part in any form without prior express written consent of the Author.

All Scriptures, unless otherwise denoted, are taken from the King James Version (KJV) Holy Bible, King James Version®, KJV® Copyright ©1973, 1978, 1984, 2011 by Biblica, Inc.® Used by permission. All rights reserved worldwide.

Scripture taken from the Holy Bible, New Living Translation (NLT), copyright © 1996, 2004, 2015 by Tyndale House Foundation. Used by permission of Tyndale House Publishers, Inc., Carol Stream, Illinois 60188. All rights reserved.

Published by Dorrette Ayensu
Typing and Encouragement: Marcia Wiltshire
Cover Design, Editing, and Final Arrangements: Denise Wilkins
Book Formatting: Crystal L. Barnes of Better Way Publishing LLC (www.crystal-barnes.com)

Printed in the United States of America

TABLE OF CONTENTS

ACKNOWLEDGEMENT iv

PREFACE v

DEDICATION vi

INTRODUCTION vii

FOREWORD by Pastor Dr. Carolyn Lewis ix

FOREWORD by Rev. Linda Demjen x

CHAPTER ONE: Uninterrupted Worship 1

CHAPTER TWO: Self-Transformation 5

CHAPTER THREE: Worship at a Higher Level 9

CHAPTER FOUR: The Many Benefits of the Worshipper 13

CHAPTER FIVE: Stay Connected 19

CHAPTER SIX: Your Journey 23

CHAPTER SEVEN: A Changed Life 27

CHAPTER EIGHT: A Transformed Worshipper 31

CHAPTER NINE: A Balanced Life 36

CHAPTER TEN: Do Worship vs Be Worship 40

NOTE FROM THE AUTHOR 46

ACKNOWLEDGEMENT

To the Holy Spirit who opened the eyes of my understanding about worship as a lifestyle. Thank you for giving me the spirit of obedience to submit. To my husband, the love of my life John Ayensu, for believing in me. A special thank you to Marcia Whilshire, who has been my greatest cheerleader. Your prayers and support kept me focused till the production of this book. In fact, thank you for your initial typing support of this book. Thank you to my brother and friend in the Lord, Pernell Hill, for all your encouragement and initial editing support. Thank you to my sister in the Lord, Denise Wilkins, who designed the cover of the book and worked with me to complete final edits, formatting, and publishing of the book. Finally, I want to say a special thank you to the "Women of Joy" group whose constant encouragement surrounded me during the completion of the book.

PREFACE

There is a place in God where worship never ceases. It is not bound by melody or confined to a moment; it is a rhythm of the heart, a sacred conversation between Creator and creation. In that place, silence becomes a song, tears become praise, and surrender becomes strength. **Uninterrupted Worship** was birthed from that sacred space, a journey of intimacy, healing, and revelation. It is my love story to God. A testimony of how His presence transforms pain into purpose and turns every broken note into a symphony of grace.

This book is an invitation to live in continual fellowship with the Lover of our soul and to move us beyond doing worship, to becoming worship itself.

DEDICATION

*For every worshipper who has ever sung through tears,
for every heart that has loved God in silence, and
for every soul learning to dwell in His presence without interruption
this book is for you.*

*May your worship become your weapon,
your love become your language,
and your life become a living altar before the Lord.*

INTRODUCTION

Jesus Christ is my Lover. I worship the love of my life continually every single day. I live to honor my Lover, my Friend, the One who loves me more than I could ever love myself.

Our love for the Lord must be expressed through worship, reverence, surrender, and total submission to the Holy Spirit. When our intimacy with God is uninterrupted, our desire for Him increases. The more we seek His love, the more His love grows within us. So let the love of God increase in your heart day by day, moment by moment.

Love requires discipline. It is a commitment to pursue the One you adore, to stay faithful, and to run the race until you win. My Lover, your Lover desires that we worship Him with excellence and with genuineness. We serve an excellent God, and only genuine worship captures His attention. For the Word declares, *"He inhabits the praises of His people."* (Psalm 22:3)

We honor and adore Him because He alone is worthy of all praise. When we begin to express our love, He comes and takes His rightful place in our midst. And as we enter the Holy Place the Holiest of Holies God leads us into our destiny, our purpose, and our divine calling.

Worship reaffirms our love for God, and His desire is to reward those who serve Him with an excellent spirit. Perfect love is found only in God; to know Him is to love like Him.

"And may you have the power to understand, as all God's people should, how wide, how long, how high, and how deep His love really is. May you experience the love of Christ,

though it is so great you will never fully understand it; then you will be filled with the fullness of life and power that comes from God." Ephesians 3:18–19

The Bible tells us that God's love is total. It reaches every corner of our lives. It is wide, covering the breadth of our experiences. It is long, stretching across the length of our days. It is high, lifting us to the heights of joy and celebration. And it is deep, reaching into the lowest valleys of despair, discouragement, and even death. That is *agape,* the perfect, unconditional love of God.

Only through Christ can this fullness of love be fully expressed. We are complete in Him, and His empowering Spirit enables us to live in oneness with Him. This fullness is cultivated through faith, prayer, praise, and continual worship. In fellowship and devotion with a sincere heart, God's great love meets us wherever we are and draws us closer to Himself.

Uninterrupted Worship is the pathway to total submission, a lifestyle of surrender and communion with God. So, ask yourself, how well do I display my love for God in the choices I make and the actions I take? Love is a decision, followed by action. God freely gave His love to us, and in return, He calls us to choose Him daily. We were created to love Him and to live in relationship with Him.

Jesus Christ's love is eternal. It never runs out, never fades, never fails. He is the Lover of your soul the source of all true love and His love spreads like fire.

"I have loved you even as the father has loved Me. Remain in My love." John 15:9

So, give Him everything you've got, your heart, your time, your voice, your worship. Let His love be your song. Let your life be His melody.

FOREWORD
Pastor Dr. Carolyn Lewis

It is with great joy and honor that I am able to witness, through my dear friend Dorrette Ayensu, the manifestation of God's glory and his faithfulness in her life, through her powerful new book, Uninterrupted Worship. I have had the privilege of knowing this great woman of God for many years. Her unwavering love for the Lord and her passion for His presence has always inspired me deeply. Dorrette's life is a true reflection of what it means to worship God in spirit and in truth not only through song, but through daily surrender and obedience. Uninterrupted Worship is more than a book; it is a divine declaration of faith, hope, courage, and determination. In these pages, Dorrette shares wisdom, revelation, and testimony that will touch the hearts of believers everywhere. I truly believe this is God's appointed time for the release of this book. The message will bring healing, deliverance, and transformation to all who read it. Prepare to encounter God in a deeper way. As you turn each page, may your spirit be refreshed, your heart be renewed, and your worship become truly uninterrupted.

With love and blessings,
Pastor Dr. Carolyn Lewis
Senior Pastor, God Empowering Kingdom Building Ministries, Inc.
Founder, God is Bigger Than Cancer Foundation, Inc.

FOREWORD
Rev. Linda Demjen

If ever there was a time that the body of Christ needed to learn how to have uninterrupted worship, it is now. This book is an excellent reminder of what we are all in need of in the times we are living in today. Dorrette is a true example of what she has written. Her book *Uninterrupted Worship* is a testimony to the truth of what we are all called to practice. She didn't get to this place without going through many trials in her faith. Her faith was being worked out with the continual love, worship, and devotion to her Lover, Jesus Christ. This book is an inspiration to us all and a great reminder of the importance of having a deep love and devotion to our Savior, Jesus Christ. This is what brings us to a place of uninterrupted worship.

Dorrette says that love requires discipline and "a commitment to pursue the One you adore, to stay faithful and to run the race until you win." Uninterrupted Worship leads believers and unbelievers to understand the importance of a relationship with Jesus so that we may finish our race well. Jesus doesn't want to just be worshipped on Sunday, but continually.

Now is the time for us to worship in truth and in spirit as Jesus taught in John 4:24. I believe this book will help every believer take their worship to another level, one that is uninterrupted throughout their day. Dorrette says, "Uninterrupted Worship goes beyond the four walls of the church. It's not restricted to the choir stand, the pulpit, or the Sunday morning service." It should be like a fountain pouring out for our spirit throughout our day and in every situation.

FOREWORD

I highly recommend this book to all who desire to know what true worship is and choose to go deeper with their relationship with Jesus. It is an inspiration in a critical time for the church. As we face persecutions, trials, and tests that could cause us to fall away, it will train us up to keep running our race to the finish line and hear the words of Jesus, "Well done, my good and faithful servant."

Rev. Linda Demjen, President
A Cup of Cold Water Ministries, Inc.

CHAPTER ONE
Uninterrupted Worship

"I will praise you as long as I live, lifting my hands to you in prayer. You satisfy me more than the richest feast; I will praise you with songs of joy." Psalm 63:4–5

UNINTERRUPTED WORSHIP—WHAT IS IT?

It is not confined to the rhythm of a Sunday service or the sound of a song. It is a lifestyle, a constant flow of communion between the believer and God. If I could describe it in one phrase, it would be this: **the life of a habitual worshipper**.

Uninterrupted Worship is worship that cannot be silenced, not by circumstances, not by people, not even by our own emotions. It is a continuous connection between the surrendered believer and the Spirit of God. It has no boundaries, no quotas, and no levels to graduate from; it is an endless well of fellowship.

When our focus is deep and our hearts are pure, our worship becomes spiritually centered. It draws us into an intimate, one-on-one connection with God. That connection strengthens our faith, increases our courage, and revives our strength.

I remember one morning as I stood in my living room, lifting my hands in praise, I suddenly felt the tangible presence of God fill the room. His peace, His love, His power all of it surrounded me like a warm blanket. In that moment, nothing else mattered. It was just me and Him. I yielded my entire being my thoughts, my emotions, even my breathing to the Holy Spirit's leading. I sensed that worship was no longer something I was doing; it had become who I was.

That day, my worship didn't end when the music stopped. It continued throughout the day while I cooked, while I worked, even as I lay down to sleep. During the night, I could still feel my spirit singing, *"Thank You, Lord, you are great!"* I turned over in bed and could hear my inner man worshipping. When I woke the next morning, those same songs were still flowing through me like a gentle stream. That is what I call **Uninterrupted Worship**. When your spirit keeps praising even while your body rests. It became clear to me that this is how God desires worship to be, not limited to a time or place, but a continual surrender of the heart.

> *"God is Spirit, and those who worship Him must worship in spirit and in truth." John 4:24*

True worship flows from a sincere heart. It is not mechanical, nor is it ritualistic. It is born out of truth, a pure recognition of who God is and what He deserves.

> *"But you are not in the flesh but in the Spirit, if indeed the Spirit of God dwells in you. Now if anyone does not have the Spirit of Christ, he is not His." Romans 8:9*

We are not to be controlled by the flesh, but by the Spirit. When the Spirit of God dwells in us fully, worship becomes as natural as breathing. It flows constantly and continually; just let it flow!

Uninterrupted Worship goes beyond the four walls of a church. It's not restricted to the choir stand, the pulpit, or the Sunday morning service. It is not confined to singing along with your favorite worship song. It is like a fountain that never runs dry, water flowing continuously, refreshing everything it touches. As this fountain pours out, we don't just offer words or melodies. We also offer our time, our gifts, our service, and our hearts. Worship that pleases God is not just sung, it is lived.

When the fountain of your worship remains open, praise will flow on good days and bad days. Circumstances will not dictate your song; the Spirit within you will. That's when you know you have moved from emotional praise to spiritual worship. When your spirit sings, *"Thank You, Lord,"* in the middle of a storm, you are walking in Uninterrupted Worship.

> *"He has given me a new song to sing, a hymn of praise to our God. Many will see what He has done and be astounded. They will put their trust in the Lord." Psalm 40:3*

We live in a time when church attendance and religious activity can easily become ritual. We tithe, we take communion, we serve, we sing yet if our hearts are not directed toward Him, those actions become empty motions. God does not want the performance of worship; He desires the posture of a surrendered heart.

> *"Praise the Lord with melodies on the lyre; make music for Him on the ten-string harp.*
> *Sing a new song of praise to Him; play skillfully on the harp and sing with joy." Psalm 33:2–3*

Worship should bring joy not obligation. It should be an overflow of love and gratitude. If your worship has become heavy, routine, or joyless, pause and ask the Holy Spirit to refresh your heart. Joy is the fruit of true worship.

Uninterrupted Worship means that whether in silence or in song, whether at home, work, or church, your heart remains in continual communion with the Father. It means your life becomes a living psalm your words, your actions, and your attitude all becoming instruments of praise.

Let your worship flow like a river that cannot be stopped. Let it fill every space you enter. Let your spirit and body become the instruments through which heaven and earth connect a living testimony of **Uninterrupted Worship.**

CHAPTER TWO
Self-Transformation

"Don't copy the behavior and customs of this world, but let God transform you into a new person by changing the way you think. Then you will learn to know God's will for you, which is good and pleasing and perfect." Romans 12:2

"Enter His gates with thanksgiving; go into His courts with praise. Give thanks to Him and bless His name." Psalm 100:4

Worship transforms a person from the inside out. It reshapes the heart, renews the mind, and realigns the spirit with God's perfect will. Through worship, God molds the believer into His likeness this is the true process of **self-transformation**. It is not self-made change; it is God-authored change.

Daily worship captures God's attention. It is in those quiet moments of adoration that grace flows and strength is renewed. This rhythm of worship becomes your purpose, your fuel, and your driving force. Worship lifts you to **Mount Zion**, the place of God's presence His holy dwelling among His people. And in that atmosphere, anything is possible.

In true worship, your time, talent, and treasures are no longer your own; they become tools to glorify God. Your mind begins to feast on His truth, your spirit grows strong, and your heart becomes courageous. Choosing a lifestyle of worship is choosing the path of transformation. That choice infuses you with boldness and stability. It makes you tenacious, firm, and confident in God's plan.

When you live this way, the enemy becomes confused. He cannot manipulate a worshipper whose heart is anchored in the Spirit. The enemy cannot understand how you continue to praise God when life seems unfair. It is the victory in your worship that endures through trials.

As the Holy Spirit renews, reeducates, and redirects your thinking, your inner nature is transformed. The old patterns fade, and a new pattern begins to emerge, one that reflects the very nature of Christ. Transformation is not cosmetic; it is spiritual. It is where God's perfect will takes effect in you, bringing out the best of who you were created to be.

As transformation takes root, your mind stabilizes. You begin to walk through different seasons of maturity with grace. Every victory becomes a celebration of His power working within you. You realize you are not just surviving you are overcoming. You are a conqueror.

Transformation and worship are intertwined. When you understand what God expects of you in worship, you enter His presence differently aware, intentional, surrendered. He welcomes you when you willingly allow Him to shape you into His image and likeness. Let this be your prayer:

"More of You, Lord, and less of me."

Worship unites you with the Spirit of God. That unity becomes your strength, your power, and your protection. It transcends human understanding and draws you deeper into divine communion.

Take a moment, even now, close your eyes and visualize yourself standing before the Father. Imagine being surrounded by angels and believers from every generation, all worshipping together in endless praise. See yourself joining that chorus, your heart lights up, your spirit free, your burdens lifted. This is what it means to rest in His presence.

SELF-TRANSFORMATION

In that sacred space, there is no fear, no anxiety, no striving only joy. His presence is real, constant, and available to you twenty-four hours a day. God welcomes your worship and delights in your rejoicing. He is pleased when you bring Him your focus, your dedication, your submission, and your faithfulness. Ask yourself: *Will I be the one who pleases Him?* Let your answer be a resounding *yes*.

When you worship, heaven moves. Your praise activates angels on your behalf. When you create a private place to be alone with Him, a sacred corner free from distractions, you create a dwelling for His glory. Remember, it's not the location that matters, but the condition of your heart.

> *"Woman, believe Me, the hour is coming when you will neither on this mountain nor in Jerusalem worship the Father. You worship what you do not know; we know what we worship, for salvation is of the Jews. But the hour is coming, and now is, when the true worshipers will worship the Father in spirit and truth; for the Father is seeking such to worship Him. God is Spirit, and those who worship Him must worship in spirit and truth." John 4:21–24*

The Father is seeking genuine worshippers, those whose hearts are wholly devoted to Him. True worship is not a performance; it is the posture of a faithful heart.

A true worshipper is someone who:

1. Lives with sincerity and loyalty to God, studying His Word and applying it daily.
2. Rejects the empty rituals of religion and embraces the living relationship of faith.
3. Carries the attributes of Christ humility, purity, and love.

We belong to Jesus. We were created to worship and glorify Him. The enemy's assignment is to distract you from your purpose. If he can keep you from prayer, from studying the Word, he slows down the process of your transformation and you cannot grow in worship. But when you press past his barriers, your worship becomes a weapon. It breaks resistance, opens revelation, and ushers in breakthrough. During one of my quiet times, the Lord spoke to my spirit and said, *"Dorrette, it is in My presence that you will receive the present."*

That word changed my life. God showed me that His gifts, His healing, His anointing, His favor, and His blessings are all found in His presence. The moment you enter that sacred place, He already has everything wrapped, prepared, and ready to be distributed.

"For there is no respect of persons with God." Romans 2:11

Whatever you need—peace, provision, strength, or deliverance—is in His presence. When your lifestyle becomes a song of praise and worship, heaven opens over you. Worship is a supernatural encounter. It is not ordinary; it is divine. So, give God your sacrifice. Give Him your *yes*.

Do you know the God you serve? When you truly know Him, your heart naturally says, "Yes to His will, yes to His way." Your *yes* becomes the sound of transformation. Each new level of worship comes with new challenges, but God already knows you are equipped to overcome them.

"I can do all things through Christ who strengthens me."
Philippians 4:13

Each challenge in His presence reveals His power. Each victory deepens your faith. As He strengthens you, rise to remain in His presence and continue to be transformed by His Spirit.

CHAPTER THREE
Worship at a Higher Level

"Happy are those who hear the joyful call to worship, for they will walk in the light of Your presence, Lord. They rejoice all day long in Your wonderful reputation; they exult in Your righteousness. You are their glorious strength; our power is based on Your favor." Psalm 89:15–17

God's desire is for His people to grow, and rise higher in faith, higher in love, higher in commitment, and higher in worship. He calls us to ascend beyond ordinary devotion and into a place of spiritual elevation. He wants us to extend, expand, and elevate our worship, being willing to sacrifice whatever is necessary to give Him our very, very best.

As your level of faith and love deepens, the Holy Spirit begins to stretch your worship. You start to sense the invitation to go higher not out of duty, but out of desire. The Scripture reminds us, *"Freely you have received; freely give."* In this higher place, worship is no longer confined to songs and Sundays. It becomes a sacred rhythm, a continual offering of love to the Lord in everything you do.

Let your love for God be the engine that drives you daily. Let worship become your holy habit, the pattern of your life. As you maintain this consistency, your commitment grows, and your heart learns to find joy in obedience. When worship becomes a lifestyle, you don't just sing it, you live it, you walk it, you speak it, you breathe it.

A Lifestyle That Builds the Kingdom

As believers, we learn to keep the spiritual flow alive in our churches, in our homes, and even in our workplaces. This kind of discipline is essential for building the Kingdom of God. But let's be honest in our daily routines, it's easy to get caught up in the rush of life. Family, work, chores, and endless responsibilities can crowd out our time with God.

Maintaining a lifestyle of worship requires intentional preparation. Before you can give God your best, you must take time to still your heart. The Lord doesn't want you burdened with the *what, when, how,* and *why* of life. He wants you to rest in the truth that you don't have to carry it all in your own strength. His strength makes the difference.

Learning to trust God strengthens your mind and prepares you to ascend to the next level. Worship at a higher level comes with reverence, order, and surrender. As your mind is renewed, your worship is elevated. God's Spirit fills you, His power flows through you, and His presence accomplishes what you could never do alone.

So, decide to trust His guidance. Maintain a worshipful attitude in all situations in joy and in hardship. Take delight in the Lord and embrace the sweetness of His presence. The time has come to take your life and worship one step higher.

To Go Higher, You Must Go Deeper

It may seem ironic, but to go higher in God, you must first go deeper. You must dig into the broken parts of yourself the insecurities, the wounds, the disappointments and allow God to heal what interrupts your worship. When you go deeper in Him your roots of faith strengthen, and your life rises to a new dimension of glory.

We are not all at the same level in our walk with God, and that's okay. Each believer is called to worship from where they are. As your worship deepens, your understanding increases, and your capacity for revelation expands. Every level introduces you to new knowledge of who God is.

> *"Much is required from those to whom much is given, and much more is required from those to whom much more has been entrusted." Luke 12:48*

If you desire more, God will give you more. If you hunger for higher dimensions of His glory, He will meet you there.

> *"Take delight in the Lord, and He will give you your heart's desires." Psalm 37:4*

To delight in the Lord means to find joy, satisfaction, and fulfillment in His presence. The more you enjoy Him, the more you understand His love. True pleasure and purpose are found in knowing God intimately, not just knowing about Him but experiencing His power and presence daily.

ENTRUSTING EVERYTHING TO HIM

> *"Commit everything you do to the Lord. Trust Him, and He will help you." Psalm 37:5*

Trust is the anchor of worship. When you entrust your life, family, and work to the Lord, you acknowledge that man's strength can only go so far. But time in God's presence reveals a deeper truth He is our help. He is our source.

When you delight in Him, your innermost desires are shaped by His will, and He grants the blessings aligned with your divine purpose. Set your affections on Him. Meditate on His Word. Make it your daily goal to please Him

> *"...they delight in doing everything the Lord wants; day and night they think about His law." Psalm 1:2*

This is the essence of uninterrupted fellowship, a continuous relationship with God, day and night. His Word becomes your meditation, His voice your guide, His presence your home. The more you immerse yourself in His Word, the more you understand His direction. You begin to recognize His voice in every decision, every transition, every challenge. Knowledge of His Word opens the door to joy unspeakable, the joy of walking in divine purpose.

CHOOSE TO DELIGHT IN THE LORD

You must come to a decision a conscious choice to delight yourself in the Lord every single day. He tells us to meditate on His Word Day and Night. Be intentional about living in His presence. Let your residence be in His glory, and your daily routine be an act of worship.

When you live this way, you will find that worship no longer depends on music, moments, or emotions. It becomes the rhythm of your spirit. And from that higher level, every part of your life becomes a song that pleases Him.

A PRAYER FOR HIGHER WORSHIP

"The one thing I ask of the Lord, the thing I seek most, is to live in the house of the Lord all the days of my life, delighting in the Lord's perfections and meditating in His temple." Psalm 27:4

PRAYER:

Lord, I give myself to You. My body is the temple of the living God. All the days of my life, I want to live in Your presence. Let me delight in Your perfections, for in Your presence there is fullness of joy, and at Your right hand are pleasures forevermore. Teach me to grow in You, to go deeper and higher, all for Your glory. Amen.

CHAPTER FOUR
The Many Benefits of the Worshipper

"The Lord shall increase you more and more, you and your children." Psalm 115:14

God is a giver of benefits. He gives us good and perfect gifts, blessings that enrich our lives and promote our well-being. These divine gifts are not just tokens of His love; they are tools that *enhance*, *strengthen*, and *elevate* us in worship. When you live a lifestyle of uninterrupted worship, you tap into the supernatural benefit of increase, an increase of peace, joy, strength, and spiritual growth.

To receive the benefits of the worshipper, you must cultivate a heart of gratitude. Gratitude sharpens your spirit and positions you for elevation. As your desire for God deepens, your worship intensifies, and your spirit becomes more attuned to His presence. Worship that is constant and sincere opens the flow of *unspeakable joy*; a joy full of glory that transforms you from the inside out.

THE JOY CONTAINER

As a worshipper, you are what I call a **Joy Container** a vessel designed to be filled with the gladness and presence of God. When your container is active and functioning properly, it lights up! The presence of God fills you from within, spilling over until it becomes visible on the outside. Every time you worship, your vessel is refilled. This divine exchange giving and receiving keeps your joy replenished again and again.

> *"I have told you this so that My joy may be in you and that your joy may be full." John 15:11*

Joy is one of the fruits of the Spirit (Galatians 5:22), and it represents a deep, abiding relationship with God. True joy transcends human emotion; it is an inward assurance birthed by the Holy Spirit. When life feels overwhelming and circumstances spiral beyond your control, fear and depression may attempt to steal your joy. But the joy given by God cannot be taken away; it can only be neglected.

If you find yourself battling depression or mental distress, remember that God, in His wisdom, has placed help within the Body of Christ. Seeking support from a trusted Christian counselor or mental health professional is not a lack of faith; it's an act of stewardship over the temple God gave you. Healing often begins when you bring your pain into the light of truth and love.

As your relationship with Jesus grows deeper, your understanding of His joy also deepens. Joy is not based on your situation; it is sustained by your connection to Him. Regardless of your highs or lows, He promises to be your strength. When your faith is tested, worship will keep your joy container full and running over.

THE BENEFIT OF A BALANCED MIND

The Lord is not only the restorer of your soul, but He is the *Balancer of your mind.* A balanced mind brings mental steadiness, emotional stability, and sound judgment. Everything begins in the mind; it's the battlefield of thoughts, feelings, and decisions.

> *"Then He opened their minds to understand the Scriptures." Luke 24:45*

Through the Holy Spirit, God opens your understanding so you can apply His Word to your life. He gives divine insight and wisdom, helping you make decisions that align with His will.

> *"You will keep him in perfect peace, whose mind is stayed on You, because he trusts in You." Isaiah 26:3*

Peace, the third fruit of the Spirit, is the stabilizing force of the believer's mind. When your thoughts remain anchored in God, peace flows freely. Speak this over yourself even now:

> *"My mind is fixed on the character of Christ. My mind is filled with the peace of God. My mind is free from fear and full of faith."*

This declaration ushers you into rest, yet, when discouragement or sadness creeps in, remember Psalm 42:5,

> *"Why am I discouraged? Why is my heart so sad? I will put my hope in God!"*

Depression is real and dangerous, a silent enemy of joy. Statistics show that more than 21 million adults in the United States experience major depression yearly, and it is the second leading cause of suicide among youth ages 12–24. But even in darkness, hope lives. When despair whispers, let worship answer. Praise lifts the broken pieces of your life and places them in God's hands, where healing begins.

> *"Though they stumble, they will not fall, for the Lord holds them by the hand." Psalm 37:24*

You are not alone. The Lord holds you steady and mends what is broken. As you worship, He replaces sorrow with song. Praise confuses the enemy and fortifies your faith. When you meditate on the goodness of Jesus, hope returns. I'm reminded of the hymn that says: *"When I think of the goodness of Jesus and what He has done for me, my soul cries out, Hallelujah! Thank God for saving me."* Even in your struggles, declare His goodness. Problems may come, but every trial carries purpose.

> *"We can rejoice, too, when we run into problems and trials, for we know that they help us learn to endure." Romans 5:3*

So, rejoice in every circumstance, rejoice! Your worship produces endurance, and endurance produces victory.

THE BENEFIT OF PURIFICATION

> *"Purify me from my sins, and I will be clean; wash me, and I will be whiter than snow." Psalm 51:7*

Purification is the benefit that cleanses the heart and renews the soul. True purity begins on the inside and flows outward, changing both behavior and character. Like David, we must humbly ask God to wash us from sin and renew a right spirit within us.

> *"Submit yourselves therefore to God. Resist the devil, and he will flee from you." James 4:7*

> *"We capture every thought and make it obedient to Christ." 2 Corinthians 10:5*

Identifying sin and turning from it are essential to the purification process. Do not live under condemnation; repentance restores relationships. Once confessed, your sin is forgiven and forgotten.

> *"As far as the east is from the west, so far has He removed our transgressions from us." Psalm 103:12*

> *"Let us cleanse ourselves from everything that can defile our body or spirit and work toward complete holiness." 2 Corinthians 7:1*

Turning from sin leads to turning toward righteousness. When you open your heart to God's love, His love purifies you. The Holy Spirit reveals what must be cleansed so that worship can flow freely. Think of purification like the building of a house. Each brick represents a part of your spiritual growth, and the cement that holds the bricks together is God's love. Without the cement the structure collapses, but with it, your foundation stands firm. God's love strengthens and unites you, holding your worship together through every storm.

THE BENEFIT OF TRANSFORMATION

> *"I beseech you therefore, brethren, by the mercies of God, that you present your bodies as a living sacrifice, holy and acceptable to God, which is your reasonable service."*
> *Romans 12:1*

Transformation is the fruit of surrender. Paul reminds us that our bodies our entire beings are to be presented to God as living sacrifices. This means dying to self and allowing Christ to live through us. Transformation is not just a change of behavior; it's a change of personality. When you yield your life completely, your desires shift, your habits align with heaven, and your mind becomes renewed.

> *"Do not copy the behavior and customs of this world, but let God transform you into a new person by changing the way you think." Romans 12:2*

Transformation affects every area of your life:

- **Your Diet:** What you consume spiritually and physically impacts your temple. The body is the temple of the Holy Spirit (1 Corinthians 6:19). Care for it with discipline. Avoid substances and habits that cloud your spirit or weaken your discernment.
- **Your Activities:** The places you go and the things you do should align with God's Word. "How can two walk together unless they agree?" (Amos 3:3). Your actions should reflect your faith.

- **Your Associations:** The people you walk with shape your spiritual direction. "Come out from among them and be separate" (2 Corinthians 6:17). Godly friends encourage, mentor, and sharpen your spirit. Choose relationships that strengthen your walk, not compromise it for *"iron sharpens iron"* (Proverbs 27:17).

Transformation molds your behavior into the character of Christ. It renews your perspective and draws you closer to the heart of God.

CLOSING REFLECTION

The benefits of the worshipper are endless joy that overflows, peace that anchors, purity that renews, and transformation that elevates. As you walk this journey, remember worship is not just something you do; it is who you are becoming. Every time you lift your hands, open your mouth, or still your heart before God, He adds another layer of His glory to your life.

So, keep your vessel full. Keep your mind balanced. Keep your heart pure. Keep your life transformed. These are the benefits of the true worshipper, and they are yours to receive every day.

CHAPTER FIVE
Stay Connected

"I am the true vine, and My Father is the gardener. He cuts off every branch in Me that bears no fruit, while every branch that does bear fruit, He prunes so that it will be even more fruitful. You are already clean because of the word I have spoken to you. Remain in Me, as I also remain in you. No branch can bear fruit by itself; it must remain in the vine. Neither can you bear fruit unless you remain in Me." John 15:1–4

Worship keeps you connected to the **Source of Life**. Jesus is the Vine; the Father is the Gardener. We, the believers, are the branches. Every branch depends entirely on the Vine for nourishment, growth, and strength. When we remain connected to Christ, life flows freely through us. But when we disconnect from Him, we begin to wither spiritually.

Just as a branch cut from its source becomes dry and lifeless, a believer who steps away from fellowship with Christ loses spiritual vitality. When we drift from prayer, neglect worship, or walk in disobedience, our fruitfulness diminishes. The Word reminds us that rebellion produces no fruit and when there is no fruit, the branch risks being cut off.

Disconnection brings weakness, fear, instability, and

powerlessness. Staying spiritually connected produces strength, courage, and clarity. The more we abide in Him, the more fruit we bear.

"Apart from Me, you can do nothing." John 15:5

I encourage you to maintain your connection with Christ. Continue in your worship, remain steadfast in your devotion, and let your roots go deep. When you stay connected, your life begins to produce divine fruit, favor, wisdom, breakthrough, and identity in Christ.

1. THE BENEFIT OF DIVINE FAVOR

"For You, Lord, will bless the righteous; with favor You will surround him as with a shield." Psalm 5:12

Favor means walking in God's grace, receiving spiritual blessings that open doors and change circumstances. His favor is not temporary; it is *lifetime favor.*

"His anger lasts only a moment, but His favor lasts a lifetime. Weeping may stay for the night, but joy comes in the morning." Psalm 30:5

When you remain connected to the Vine, favor follows you. It positions you in places you could not reach on your own. It brings opportunities, divine connections, and protection. Scripture declares that we can "find favor with both God and man" (*Proverbs 3:4*). God's promises are sure what He declares, He delivers.

2. THE BENEFIT OF GODLY WISDOM

"The fear of the Lord is the beginning of wisdom." Proverbs 9:10

Wisdom is one of God's hidden treasures a divine mystery revealed only to those who seek Him. It cannot be found apart from relationship. Those who remain connected to the Vine receive insight, discernment, and divine understanding.

Wisdom allows you to make godly decisions even in difficult circumstances. It guides your thoughts, shapes your choices, and protects your path. True wisdom flows from reverence for God, it refines your behavior and aligns your life with righteousness.

> *"If any of you lacks wisdom, let him ask of God, who gives to all liberally and without reproach." James 1:5*

3. THE BENEFIT OF SPIRITUAL BREAKTHROUGH

> *"But you will receive power when the Holy Spirit comes upon you." Acts 1:8*

God prepares breakthroughs for those who remain steadfast in Him. The same power that worked in the early church is still at work in us today. Purity, unity, boldness, love, and humility—these are the hallmarks of Spirit-led believers.

Breakthroughs come when worship and obedience intersect. When your faith is tested, your worship becomes the weapon that breaks chains. Through trials, temptations, and disappointments, God promises never to leave you.

> *"In all these things we are more than conquerors through Him who loved us." Romans 8:37*

Your breakthrough ushers in a season of harvest, a time when favor flows, peace reigns, and victory silences every storm.

4. THE BENEFIT OF YOUR IDENTITY IN CHRIST

Many people today are struggling to discover who they are. The world's confusion about identity has left many searching for worth in temporary things. But as believers, our identity is secure in Christ.

> *"And we all, who with unveiled faces contemplate the Lord's glory, are being transformed into His image with ever-increasing glory, which comes from the Lord, who is the*

Spirit." 2 Corinthians 3:18

Your true identity is found in Him. When you know who you belong to, insecurity loses its grip. You are not defined by your past, your failures, or your surroundings; you are defined by God's Word.

"For we are God's masterpiece. He has created us anew in Christ Jesus, so that we can do the good things He planned for us long ago." Ephesians 2:10

You are marked by the Holy Spirit, sealed, chosen, and set apart. God has placed His divine approval upon your life. You are His workmanship, and nothing can separate you from His love.

STAYING CONNECTED IN DAILY LIFE

Staying connected to the Vine requires daily intention. You cannot live off yesterday's worship or last week's prayer. Relationship with God thrives through consistency.

Spend time in His presence. Stay rooted in the Word. Surround yourself with other believers who sharpen your faith. When storms come, don't disconnect, dig deeper. Pruning may hurt, but it's necessary for growth. God removes what hinders so He can multiply what helps.

When you remain in Christ, fruitfulness is guaranteed. You will experience divine favor, supernatural wisdom, spiritual breakthroughs, and an unshakable identity in Him. So, stay connected, remain in the Vine. Let His life flow through you daily and watch how everything connected to you begins to grow.

"Those who are planted in the house of the Lord shall flourish in the courts of our God." Psalm 92:13

CHAPTER SIX
Your Journey

"For I know the plans I have for you," says the Lord. "They are plans for good and not for disaster, to give you a future and a hope." Jeremiah 29:11

When Jeremiah wrote this promise to the Jews exiled in Babylon, he was sending letters of hope to a broken people. Jerusalem had fallen. Their homes were gone. Their hearts were heavy. Yet in the middle of captivity, God spoke of *plans*, not punishment. He reminded them that their story wasn't over. After seventy long years, restoration would come.

Worship, in many ways, is like that journey through exile. It leads you into unknown places and seasons that test your patience and faith. But in every turn, every pause, and every wilderness moment, God's plan remains good. Your journey is not random; it is *intentional*. It is God's mission, His map for your life.

GUIDED BY THE MASTER PLANNER

"I will guide you along the best pathway for your life. I will advise you and watch over you." Psalm 32:8

What a comfort to know that your journey is under divine supervision. God Himself the Creator of time, space, and destiny is guiding your path. You are not wandering aimlessly. You are walking in purpose.

He promises to advise you and watch over you. That means He gives counsel, wisdom, and direction for each step. His Word declares that He gives His angels charge over you, to guard and protect you in all your ways (Psalm 91:11). You are never traveling alone. Heaven monitors your movements. The Father has charted your course and established every destination point before you arrive.

Sometimes the road will twist unexpectedly; sometimes the climb feels steep. But remember God sees the end from the beginning. What looks uncertain to you is perfectly clear to Him. So do not fear. Trust His hand when you cannot trace His plan. Let the Holy Spirit be your compass. He knows where the detours lead, where the hidden blessings are buried, and where the next miracle will unfold. His promises are true. His relationship with you is everlasting. His protection is constant, and your life is secure in Him.

THE DISCIPLINE OF FOCUS AND OBEDIENCE

"Therefore, be careful to do as the Lord your God has commanded you; do not turn aside to the right or to the left. Walk in all the ways that the Lord your God has commanded you, that you may live and that it may be well with you, and that you may prolong your days in the land which you shall possess."
Deuteronomy 5:32–33

Every journey with God requires focus. The enemy's strategy is distraction to make you turn right or left when you should be walking straight ahead. Life demands relationships, and even good things can pull your attention away from God's voice. But obedience keeps you aligned. It lengthens your days, prospers your path, and brings you safely into the land of promise. Your faithfulness is what keeps heaven's plan unfolding.

God has already provided everything you need to survive and

thrive on this journey. Don't lose heart. Don't give up. Keep walking even when the road feels long. Stay patient, stay humble, and keep your spiritual eyes fixed on Jesus.

> **Say this aloud:** *"I am on a worship journey. Where He leads me, I will follow. I will go with Him all the way, and I will grow with Him all the way."*

GROWING THROUGH THE JOURNEY

I've learned from my own life that this journey isn't just about **going** with God, it's about **growing** with Him. Growth doesn't always happen in comfort; it often happens in conflict, correction, and surrender.

There were seasons when I didn't know where God was taking me. I couldn't see what He was doing, but I could sense His presence guiding me through every challenge. Over time, I realized: I don't need to know the route, as long as I know the Guide. Every day with Jesus truly becomes sweeter than the day before. Even when life brings uncertainty, the presence of the Lord brings peace. The more I fix my eyes on Him, the more I experience His faithfulness. My obedience to Him has produced the kind of joy the world cannot give, and a relationship that only He could design.

YOUR JOURNEY IS PART OF HIS PLAN

God loves you deeply. You are not forgotten. You are not off schedule. You are exactly where you need to be for Him to work out His divine purpose in your life. His invitation is simple yet profound: *Follow Me.* Live a life that pleases Him. Trust His timing. Worship through the waiting. His goodness and mercy are not seasonal; they are lifelong companions that follow you every step of the way (Psalm 23.6). He refuses to abandon you; you are *in* His plan. And in your **going**, He wants you to keep **growing**.

Each level of growth reveals a new side of God's character. You will learn His faithfulness in suffering, His power in weakness, His peace in chaos, and His joy in obedience. So, walk boldly. Keep worshiping. Keep trusting. Every valley, every detour, every climb is part of your spiritual pilgrimage toward promise. The journey is not about the destination alone; it's about becoming who God designed you to be along the way.

> *"The steps of a good man are ordered by the Lord, and He delights in his way." Psalm 37:23*

A Final Word for the Worship Journey

Your worship journey is a living testimony. It tells the world that you trust God's direction more than your own. It says that even when the path feels uncertain, your faith remains unshaken. Let your story remind others that every believer is on a journey unique in route but united in purpose. We are all travelers being shaped, tested, and refined by the hand of the Master.

> *"Keep moving forward with gratitude in your heart and worship on your lips. The One who began this good work in you will be faithful to complete it." Philippians 1:6*

Your journey with God is not random; it's revelatory. It reveals who He is, and in turn, who you are in Him. So, trust the process, enjoy the path, and never forget: **the destination is His presence.**

CHAPTER SEVEN
A Changed Life

"Therefore, if anyone is in Christ, he is a new creation; old things have passed away; behold, all things have become new."
2 Corinthians 5:17

In today's world, many view lifestyles and behaviors as "normal" or "acceptable." But, through a moral or biblical lens, God's Word has never changed, truth still stands. I know this from experience. There was a season in my life when I walked far from the principles of my faith. Out of curiosity, I stepped into a lifestyle that I knew was not God's best for me. For eight long years, I lived in a relationship that was toxic, jealous, and controlling, yet I stayed, hoping somehow it would get better. Deep down inside, I knew something was missing. I was trapped in a cage of my own making; bound by emotions I could not control.

Even though I knew right from wrong, I chose to ignore that still, small voice, but God's grace never stopped calling. No matter how far I drifted, His love was relentless. One day, broken and tired, I cried out, *"Lord, change my desires to align with Yours. I want to live a life that pleases You. I want a godly husband. I want Your plan, not mine."* That desperate prayer became the doorway to my transformation.

Transformation doesn't happen overnight; it's a process. Inner change begins when you allow God to reach into the hidden places of your heart. He patiently reshapes you, renews your mind, and redirects your desires toward His will.

For me, change began with surrender. I had to change my language, my appearance, my thinking, and my entire outlook on life. I started building a prayer life, spending time in God's Word, and learning to listen to His Spirit. Slowly, my old habits faded, and my heart began to hunger for holiness.

I fell in love with Jesus all over again more deeply each day. Every morning became an opportunity to walk in newness. I began to see myself not as who I *was*, but as who God was creating me to *be*.

> *"And do not be conformed to this world but be transformed by the renewing of your mind." Romans 12:2*

Inner change leads to faithful action. When God begins to change your heart, your behavior follows. Something inside must die so something better can be born. Hold on during the process don't rush it. Your change is coming. Even now, God is doing a work in you that eyes cannot see.

> *"Now to Him who is able to do exceedingly abundantly above all that we ask or think…" Ephesians 3:20*

There are seasons when God calls you to separate from people, places, and patterns that keep you bound. To walk in freedom, I had to change my surroundings my environment, my friendships, even some family dynamics.

If you want to succeed in what God is calling you to do, you must surround yourself with people who strengthen your spirit, not feed your struggle. You must dwell in an atmosphere that feeds your faith.

> *"They are not of the world, even as I am not of the world." John 17:16*

A Changed Life

It also matters where you worship. If you are not in a Bible-believing, Spirit-filled church that teaches the unchanging truth of God's Word, ask the Lord to guide you to one. Move beyond religious routine and find a fellowship of believers who will help you grow in grace and truth.

> *"The Lord, your Redeemer, the Holy One of Israel, says: I am the Lord your God, who teaches you what is good and leads you along the path you should follow." Isaiah 48:17*

When you follow God fully not partially, He will guide you to the right place, at the right time, for the right purpose. He will go before you, rearranging circumstances to your advantage. Your obedience is the key that unlocks divine direction.

When you surrender to God's will, you begin to prosper not just spiritually, but in every area of life. He teaches you to walk in wisdom, to steward your resources, and to trust Him with your finances.

> *"But remember the Lord your God, for it is He who gives you power to get wealth." Deuteronomy 8:18*

God's blessing is tied to obedience. When your heart is right, provision follows. He looks not at your outward appearance but at the posture of your heart. Be honest with God, he already sees the real you; that is where change begins.

Uninterrupted worship keeps your spirit aligned with His will. When life feels heavy, answer your struggles with praise. Let your worship be the weapon that breaks every chain. Praise is not just a song; it's a declaration of victory before the battle is even over.

> *"The righteous cry out, and the Lord hears, and delivers them out of all their troubles." Psalm 34:17*

Jesus is both the **Purifier** and the **Sanctifier**. He cleanses you from all unrighteousness, renews your mind, and sets you apart for His glory.

"If we confess our sins, He is faithful and just to forgive us our sins and to cleanse us from all unrighteousness."
1 John 1:9

Thanks be to God who gives us everything we need for life and godliness through Christ Jesus. He doesn't just forgive, He transforms. He replaces guilt with grace, shame with strength, and emptiness with joy.

A Prayer for a Changed Life

Lord, cleanse me from the inside out. Continue the process of change within me. Give me healthy thoughts and pure motives so that everything I do will please You. Filter my mind through Your Word and renew my spirit daily. Let my desires align with Yours, and let my life reflect Your glory. Thank You for loving me enough to change me. Thank You for giving me a new identity in You. I receive Your transforming power, and I walk boldly in the freedom You've provided. In Jesus' name, Amen.

A Final Word

A changed life is not the absence of struggle; it is the presence of God's strength in the middle of it. Transformation is a daily decision to keep walking in the direction of destiny. Every time you say "yes" to God, the old you lose its grip a little more. Every act of obedience reshapes your story. Every moment of worship pulls you closer to His will. You don't have to live bound by yesterday. You are living proof that God still changes lives. So, lift your hands, lift your heart, and declare: *"Thank You, Lord, for a changed life. I believe it, and I receive it."*

CHAPTER EIGHT
A Transformed Worshipper

"And be not conformed to this world: but be ye transformed by the renewing of your mind, that ye may prove what is that good, and acceptable, and perfect, will of God."
Romans 12:2

God is zealous for our worship and jealous for our love. When we truly love Him, that love begins to change us. It transforms the way we think, see, and live. A renewed mind is the gateway to discovering God's perfect will for our lives, what is good, acceptable, and pleasing in His sight.

When Jesus entered the temple in Jerusalem during Passover, He found merchants buying, selling, and exchanging money. What was meant to be a sacred space, a *House of Prayer*, had been turned into a den of thieves. In righteous anger, Jesus overturned their tables and declared,

"My Temple shall be called a house of prayer for all nations."
Matthew 21:12–13

In the same way, our bodies are temples of the Holy Spirit (1 Corinthians 6:19). When we fill our lives with the clutter of sin, compromise, and distractions, we dishonor the sacred dwelling of God within us. Transformation begins when we allow the Holy Spirit to cleanse our inner temple to overturn everything that doesn't belong. We must die daily to "fleshy desires" so we can live to please God.

> *"If anyone desires to come after Me, let him deny himself, and take up his cross daily, and follow Me." Luke 9:23*

To take up your cross is to sacrifice your will for God's will. It's choosing obedience over comfort. It's surrendering your agenda for His purpose. This is the life of a *transformed worshipper.* **Be a God Chaser, not a Man Pleaser.**

A transformed worshipper doesn't chase applause or acceptance; they chase after God. The Holy Spirit is constantly drawing us into deeper levels of worship, faith, and intimacy with Him. I remember one powerful night of all-night prayer when the Spirit of God filled the room. We worshipped until the presence of the Lord was almost tangible. In that moment, God spoke to me clearly: *"I will give you the unction to function."* I didn't understand it at first, but my pastor explained, *"God is anointing you to do His work."*

That phrase changed me. The *unction to function* means divine empowerment, the supernatural ability to do what God has called you to do. Transformation isn't just about change; it's about divine enablement. When you know the **WHO** (Jesus), you understand the **WHY** (His faithfulness) behind your worship.

The Lord is calling His people to a higher level of worship from mere participation to personal transformation. He wants us to worship from a renewed mind and a purified heart. When you press into His presence that secret place of *Psalm 91:1* your worship becomes uninterrupted and unshakeable. True worship validates your authenticity in God. It's not performance; it's proof of your intimacy.

Transformation isn't just visible in what you *say* it's revealed in how you *live.* It's reflected in your humility, your patience, your giving, your service, and your willingness to love others.

EIGHT MARKS OF A TRANSFORMED WORSHIPPER

1. A Consistent Prayer Life

Prayer is the heartbeat of a transformed life. It keeps your spirit alive and your joy intact.

> *"...for the joy of the LORD is your strength." Nehemiah 8:10*

When prayer fades, joy fades. When prayer flows, strength grows.

2. A Generous Heart

True worshippers are givers of their time, talents, and treasures. Giving isn't a burden; it's a privilege. A willing heart opens the door for God's blessings to flow.

> *"It is more blessed to give than to receive." Acts 20:35*

3. The Heart of God

> *"...that Christ may dwell in your hearts through faith; that you, being rooted and grounded in love, may be able to comprehend... the love of Christ which passes knowledge." Ephesians 3:17–19*

Jesus isn't a guest. He's the rightful owner of your heart. His love roots you deeply, making you strong, stable, and secure.

4. Endurance Under Trial

> *"Blessed is the man that endureth temptation: for when he is tried, he shall receive the crown of life." James 1:12*

Every test is preparation for promotion. When you endure, you prove your faith and position yourself for a crown of victory.

5. An Intercessor's Spirit

> *"I exhort therefore, that first of all, supplications, prayers, intercessions, and giving of thanks, be made for all men." 1 Timothy 2:1*

A transformed worshipper prays not only for themselves but for others. Intercession expands your heart to carry the burdens of God's people and aligns you with His compassion.

6. A Life Led by the Holy Spirit

Transformation means surrendering control. You begin to live through the leading of the Holy Spirit, guided by His Word and grace. The Spirit becomes your teacher, your comforter, and your guide into truth.

7. A Personal Relationship with God

Worship isn't corporate first; it's personal. I call Him *"Daddy God"* because our relationship is intimate. I don't need music or a crowd to find Him. My worship is constant, and my gratitude is unending. In His presence, I find fullness of joy and strength for every season.

8. A Worship That Moves Heaven

Worship moves the hand of God. It activates favor and shifts atmospheres. You don't have to wait for a Sunday service or a choir to sing your song; your heart can sing anywhere, anytime. Ask, seek, and knock, and doors will open (Matthew 7:7). The transformed worshipper doesn't just visit God's presence; they *abide* there. Their worship becomes a way of life, a continual offering of love, faith, and obedience.

God's desire is for us to be carriers of His glory, a living temple where His Spirit dwells and works through us daily. When you are transformed, your worship changes. When your worship changes, your world changes.

A Closing Prayer

Father, thank You for transforming me from the inside out. Renew my mind daily and make me a vessel of true worship. Cleanse my heart and fill my life with Your presence. Let my thoughts, words, and actions reflect Your glory. Give me the unction to function and the power to walk in Your purpose. I surrender all to You. Let my worship be uninterrupted, authentic, and alive.

In Jesus's name, Amen.

CHAPTER NINE
A Balanced Life

"...I have learned, in whatsoever state I am, therewith to be content. I know both how to be abased, and I know how to abound: everywhere and in all things, I am instructed both to be full and to be hungry, both to abound and to suffer need. I can do all things through Christ which strengtheneth me."
Philippians 4:11–13

There was a time in my life when balance was the last thing on my mind. I worked hard during the day and lived for the world at night. After work, my friends and I would meet up at the bars. They'd drink alcohol while I sipped on virgin strawberry daiquiris, and together we'd smoke marijuana, laugh, and chase whatever happiness the night offered.

I had moved out on my own, free from anyone's rules or expectations. I thought independence meant freedom. But in reality, I was bound by pride, disobedience, and the illusion that I was in control. Church wasn't even a thought in my mind. My happiness was built on the next thrill, not on truth.

One day, I reached a breaking point. I looked at my life and said, *"Stop. Think. Turn."* My spiritual eyes began to open, and I realized that what I was searching for in all the wrong places was found only in

God. I decided to accept what God allows and desire what God desires for my life. That decision became the beginning of balance.

Paul said, "In whatever state I am, be content." (vs11)

Contentment is not passive acceptance; it is a **peaceful confidence** in God's sovereignty. It's a learned posture, a quiet heart that trusts God's wisdom more than its own understanding.

"For My thoughts are not your thoughts, neither are your ways My ways, saith the LORD." Isaiah 55:8–9

When we rely on our own way of thinking, we create imbalance. When we lean into God's way, He steadies our steps. So many of us come to God looking for peace, love, and happiness. Yet, true peace doesn't come from striving, it comes from surrender. I spent years *trying,* trying to fix things, trying to please people, trying to make life work my way. But all that trying only led to frustration and exhaustion. When we live in the cycle of "trying," we are living out of **our own strength**, not God's. The goal is to **stop striving and start trusting**. Each test in life is an invitation to learn, not to fail. God's tests aren't meant to break you they're meant to shape you.

Paul said, *"I know both how to be abased and how to abound."* To be **abased** means to be humbled, brought low, stripped of pride and independence so that dependence on God can be restored.

I remember when I was living in Nassau, Bahamas, in a relationship my mother strongly disapproved of. My pride wouldn't let me listen. When she told me I had to leave, I defiantly said, *"I will not change!"* That pride led me to move to New York, where I lived freely or so I thought.

That relationship lasted eight years, but by the end, it turned abusive and toxic. She slept with a knife beside her pillow. I knew it was time to escape. God used that experience to humble me. My disobedience brought me low, but His grace lifted me up.

UNINTERRUPTED WORSHIP

"God resists the proud but gives grace to the humble."
James 4:6

That was my "abasing." I had to lose myself to find God again. When the scales fell from my eyes, I could finally see that my freedom apart from God was bondage, but my surrender to Him was true liberty.

From there, I began to **abound** not in possessions or status, but in peace, grace, and spiritual abundance. I joined a local church, became part of the worship team, and found my voice again not just as a singer, but as a worshipper. I began traveling, singing, leading, and ministering. My joy returned. My balance was restored.

"But let patience have her perfect work, that ye may be perfect and entire, wanting nothing." James 1:4

Patience is not weakness it's spiritual endurance. When life gets difficult, patience anchors your soul. Even in the valley of the shadow of death, you can say,

"I will fear no evil, for You are with me; Your rod and Your staff, they comfort me." Psalm 23:4

The perfect work of God matures you. It balances your emotions, strengthens your spirit, and keeps you complete lacking nothing.

One Sunday, I visited a church where the pastor preached from *Jeremiah 8:7*:

"Even the stork in the sky knows her appointed seasons, and the dove, the swift, and the thrush observe the time of their migration. But My people do not know the requirements of the Lord."

The pastor explained that birds know *when* to move they sense the right time because they follow the light. If you put them in darkness and turn on a light, they will immediately face toward it. Then he said something that ignited my spirit: *"The birds know when to move, but*

God's people often miss their timing because they've stopped following the true Light."

He continued: *"Our balance is in our ear."*

That revelation struck me deeply. Spiritually and physically our **balance** depends on what we hear. Faith comes by hearing (Romans 10:17). So, if we want to stay balanced, we must be careful about what and who we listen to. When you fill your ears with negativity, gossip, or doubt, your spiritual equilibrium is disrupted. But when you tune your ear to God's Word, your spirit stabilizes. His voice becomes your compass.

Many in the Church today are spiritually disoriented confused, unclear, and off course. Why? Because they've replaced relationship with routine and traded revelation for religion. Jesus said, *"I am the Light of the world."* When we fix our eyes on Him, balance is restored. Worship aligns us. The Word anchors us. The Spirit guides us.

When God changes your life, He doesn't erase your personality He redeems it. Your gifts, your uniqueness, your voice all of it becomes a tool for His glory. Effective living isn't measured by what we *achieve*, but by what we *overcome* to achieve it. Every time you rise from failure, you build balance. Every time you surrender, you grow stronger. An effective worshipper learns from the Master and builds upon His work. Jesus said, *"Greater works than these shall you do."* (John 14:12) You are called to continue what He began to let your worship, your faith, and your obedience reveal His greatness in the earth

CHAPTER TEN
Do Worship vs Be Worship

"How then shall they call on Him in whom they have not believed? And how shall they believe in Him of whom they have not heard? And how shall they hear without a preacher?"
Romans 10:14–15

Every Sunday, churches all over the world are filled with people who have gathered to worship God. But within those gatherings, there are different kinds of worshippers, each standing at a different point on their spiritual journey.

1. **The Invited Guest** – These are the ones who are experiencing church for the first time. They may have little to no knowledge of what to expect, but something has drawn them to the House of God curiosity, desperation, or divine appointment.
2. **The Spectator** – These individuals come merely to observe. They attend out of routine, obligation, or social connection, but their hearts remain disengaged.
3. **The "Do Worshippers"** – These worshippers *do* worship. They participate with sincerity, but their worship is often tied to emotions and circumstances. When life feels heavy and the music begins to stir their hearts, they lift their

hands, tears fall, and they feel something shift, but it is temporary. Their worship happens *in the moment* but doesn't yet extend into *the lifestyle.*
4. **The "Be Worshippers"** – These are those who have gone beyond the emotional experience. They have become living worship. Their relationship with God is consistent, intimate, and deeply rooted. Worship flows through every area of their lives in their thoughts, choices, conversations, and conduct.

As a little girl, I was raised in church. My grandmother made sure I was in Sunday services, choir practice, and youth programs. I loved the singing, the atmosphere, and the feeling of being in God's presence. Worship was being planted in my heart, even though I didn't fully understand it yet.

As I grew older, however, the world began to call. Slowly, my desire for worldly pleasures outweighed my commitment to church. I drifted but never completely walked away. I would attend services occasionally, hear the Word, feel convicted, and find myself at the altar in tears. In those moments, I *did worship.* My emotions were moved. My heart longed to change. But when the service ended, I went back to the same lifestyle.

> *"For what I am doing, I do not understand. For what I will to do, that I do not practice; but what I hate, that I do."*
> *Romans 7:15*

That was me stuck in a cycle of *doing worship* but not *being transformed by worship.* It took twenty years of living this way before I realized I needed more than a temporary emotional release. I needed a **renewed mind** and a **restored relationship.** I needed to stop "doing" worship and start "being" worship.

When I finally surrendered my life to God, everything changed. I began to understand Isaiah 26:3 *"You will keep him in perfect peace whose mind is stayed on You."*

Worship became my weapon and my refuge. When temptation came, I worshipped my way out of it. When sorrow came, I praised my way through it. When confusion arose, I prayed my way back to peace. My worship stopped being reactionary it became relational.

I remember crying out one day, *"My God, my Lover, who loves me just as I am, fill my heart with Your peace and joy. Make me free by Your grace. You are the reason I live."* As I worshipped, His presence embraced me. Suddenly, I was led to Isaiah 43:1:

> *"But now, O Jacob, listen to the LORD who created you. O Israel, the one who formed you says, 'Do not be afraid, for I have ransomed you. I have called you by name; you are mine.'"*

And the Lord whispered to my spirit, *"Replace Jacob with your name."* I heard Him say, *"Dorrette, I have called you by name. You are mine."* Tears streamed down my face as the weight of His love broke me open. I no longer wondered where I stood with God. He had claimed me as His own. That moment marked the birth of a **Be Worshipper** one who doesn't just sing about Him but lives for Him.

> *"I will bless the Lord at all times; His praise shall continually be in my mouth. My soul shall make its boast in the Lord; The humble shall hear of it and be glad. Oh, magnify the Lord with me, and let us exalt His name together." Psalm 34:1–3*

The average believer begins their walk by *praising* their way into worship. Praise opens the door, but worship keeps you in the room. King David understood this well. As a young shepherd, he spent countless hours in the fields singing praises to God. Over time, his relationship deepened from praise to worship, from music to intimacy. David experienced triumphs and failures, yet his heart always turned back toward God.

In *Acts 13:22,* the Lord called David *"a man after My own heart."*

David wasn't perfect he was passionate, repentant, and real. His honesty and humility before God made him a *Be Worshipper*.

When David sinned, he repented. When he was victorious, he worshipped. When he was afraid, he sang. His life was an open book before God. That is the essence of being worship, transparency before the One who sees all.

> *"He that believeth on Me, as the Scripture hath said, out of his belly shall flow rivers of living water." John 7:38*

True worship is not an occasional act; it is a constant flow. When you *become* worship, rivers of living water flow out of you refreshing others, glorifying God, and bringing life wherever you go.

DO WORSHIP VS. BE WORSHIP

DO WORSHIP	BE WORSHIP
Emotionally driven	Spiritually anchored
Seasonal or circumstantial	Consistent and continual
Seeks comfort	Seeks communion
Focuses on self	Focuses on God
Experiences God	Lives in God
Feels His presence occasionally	Carries His presence daily

The "Do Worshipper" lifts their hands *in moments*. The "Be Worshipper" *lifts their life* before God daily. The difference is not in the song; it's in the surrender.

LET WORSHIP FLOW

Becoming a "Be Worshipper" means letting your worship flow freely through every area of your life. It's not just about what happens in church, but how you speak, how you love, how you forgive, and how you serve.

When you *be* worship, your life becomes a living psalm. Your very presence carries peace. Your faith inspires others. Your obedience becomes an offering. So, lift your heart, not just your hands. Let your lifestyle sing louder than your voice. Be the worship that Heaven recognizes.

> *"Lord, make me more than a worshipper in the moment. Make me a living sanctuary a vessel of praise. Let my life glorify You when no one is watching. Let my worship flow, unbroken, unending, unstoppable.*

A Final Charge To The Worshipper

Let God's Spirit impart *balance* and *soundness of mind*. Let Him center your heart, settle your spirit, and steady your steps. Live a life of **Uninterrupted Worship,** constant, consistent, and Christ-centered. Let God's worshippers arise and take their place. Be a habitual worshipper who is moved by devotion, and not one who is moved by emotion. It's never too late to begin again.

*For every worshipper who has ever felt unseen
yet kept singing anyway
for every heart that has loved God through
tears, silence, and storms
this book is for you.
May your worship never be interrupted, and
may His presence forever be your home.*

NOTE FROM THE AUTHOR

This book holds a very special place in my heart. It is a privilege to be called by God to write a book that reveals the depth of His heart for *Uninterrupted Worship*. From the time I was a little girl, I loved singing songs about God. Whether I was in church, at school, or somewhere in my community, someone would always call on me to sing. It was as though singing became my first language of love; a way to feel God's presence even before I truly understood it. The ministry leaders of my church recognized the gift that rested upon my life and encouraged me to pursue it. Looking back, I see now that those early moments were not just performances; they were the beginning of my calling, the first whispers of what would become my lifelong ministry as a worship leader. I grew by the spirit of the Lord to understand how to "be worship" and not just "do worship."

I remember a time in prayer when the Lord gave me a simple yet powerful vision. In the spirit, I saw an open faucet with water flowing endlessly. I understood that if I turned the handle, the water would stop, but if I allowed it to remain open, the flow would continue without interruption. In that moment, God revealed something profound: this is what a lifestyle of Uninterrupted Worship looks like.

NOTE FROM THE AUTHOR

"Give, and it will be given to you: good measure, pressed down, shaken together, and running over, will be poured into your lap." Luke 6:38

As I reflected on the vision, I began to see how the flow of water represents our worship. We each hold the faucet in our hands. We can choose to keep it open allowing our worship, our giving, our time, and our devotion to flow freely, or we can close it off. The more we release the more God pours back into us. Worship is reciprocal: as we give of ourselves, heaven responds with an overflow, pressed down, shaken together, and running over.

I am deeply grateful that you have taken the time to walk with me through this journey of *Uninterrupted Worship*. This journey is not meant to end here, it continues for all eternity. With a humble heart, I have given God my best and He has transformed me from the inside out.

Every believer was created to worship. I urge you to cultivate your personal relationship with God. Let your worship take you there. Let the Holy Spirit lead you into deeper intimacy. Let your cry of worship become a place where He delights to dwell. Keep the fire of worship burning. Keep your balance through prayer, patience, and perseverance. And above all, keep your focus on Jesus, He is the true Light.

"Rejoice in the Lord always; again, I say, rejoice."
Philippians 4:4

Made in the USA
Coppell, TX
22 February 2026